P9-DCJ-351

Horse POWER

Fire HORSES

by Margaret Fetty

Consultant: Geoffrey N. Stein
Firefighting Historian

BEARPORT PUBLISHING

New York, New York

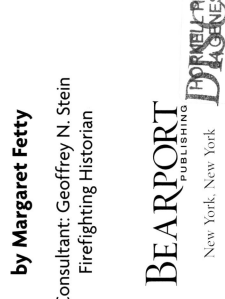

Credits

Cover and Title Page, © Dave & Barbara Hubert; 4, © Fredericton Firefighters Museum, New Brunswick; 5, © Fredericton Firefighters Museum, New Brunswick; 6, © Florida Photographic Collection; 7, © San Diego Historical Society (# 3014); 8, © Sheila Terry/SCIENCE PHOTO LIBRARY/ Photo Researchers, Inc; 9, © Minnesota Historical Society/CORBIS; 10, © Denver Public Library, Western History Collection, X-6223; 11, © Bettmann/CORBIS; 12, © Glenbow Archives NA-2854-107; 13, © Denver Public Library, Western History Collection, X-29624; 14, © Chris Jones/Corbis; 15, © Hulton-Deutsch Collection/CORBIS; 16, © Topical Press Agency/Getty Image; 17, © The Maryland Historical Society; 18, © SuperStock, Inc./SuperStock; 19, © Brown Brothers; 20, © Dave & Barbara Hubert; 21, © Daily News Pix; 22, © Collection of George F. Getz, Jr./NHFF; 23, © Photo by Lisa Dutton, courtesy of Toledo Fire Museum; 24, © San Diego Historical Society (# 3050); 25, © Melvin E. Diemer/Wisconsin Historical Society/Courtesy Everett Collection; 26, © Albert Dreyfus/ CORBIS; 27, © Glenbow Archives NA-2003-97; 29T, © Robert Maier/Animals Animals-Earth Scenes; 29C, © Bob Langrish/Animals Animals-Earth Scenes; 29B, © Leonard Rue Enterprises/Animals Animals-Earth Scenes.

Publisher: Kenn Goin
Senior Editor: Lisa Wiseman
Creative Director: Spencer Brinker
Photo Researcher: Amy Dunleavy
Original Design: Stacey May

Library of Congress Cataloging-in-Publication Data

Fetty, Margaret.
Fire horses / by Margaret Fetty.
   p. cm. — (Horse power)
Includes bibliographical references.
ISBN-13: 978-1-59716-626-3 (library binding)
ISBN-10: 1-59716-626-X (library binding)
1. Draft horses—Juvenile literature. I. Title.

SF311.F48 2008
636.1'5—dc22

                                    2007036275

10 9 8 7 6 5 4 3 2 1

Contents

Fire!

A loud sound broke the silence of the firehouse. It was the fire alarm. A building was on fire in Fredericton, New Brunswick, Canada. The firemen had to hurry!

Hugh O'Neill rushed to the front of the building. He tugged on a metal ring on the floor. It opened the doors to the **stall** at the back of the firehouse. Two fire horses ran out excitedly and stopped in front of the **ladder truck**.

Fire horses Doll (front) and Bill (back) in front of their fire station in Fredericton, New Brunswick, Canada, in 1937

O'Neill **hitched** the animals to the truck and climbed up into the seat. Grabbing the **reins,** O'Neill shouted to the horses, "Let's go, Bill and Doll! We have to stop that fire!" They raced out the front door.

After the alarm sounded, the firemen and their horses were able to leave the firehouse in less than 30 seconds.

Doll (left) and Bill (right) being harnessed

Saving a City

Bill and Doll **galloped** along the city streets. Doll slowed down as they climbed a hill. Bill turned his head and nipped her neck. He wanted her to run faster. Bill knew their job was important. A fire could spread quickly and cause a lot of damage.

Firefighters stand in front of a hose wagon

There were different kinds of fire trucks and wagons. Bill and Doll pulled a truck that held ladders. Some wagons carried water hoses.

Finally, they arrived at the scene. Thanks to Bill and Doll's speed, the fire had not spread too far. The horses bravely pulled the truck near the red-hot flames. Once the ladders were unloaded, a fireman moved Bill and Doll away from the fire. They waited **patiently** as the firemen battled the blaze. At last, the flames were out. The city was safe!

Some trucks carried special ladders that could be raised three stories into the air. They could hold up to five men at a time.

Four-Footed Firemen

Before fire horses like Bill and Doll, people battled fires very differently. In the 1600s, men would form a line near a water source and pass along buckets of water. The person closest to the fire would dump the water on it.

Then in the 1700s, men pulled heavy fire equipment by hand to fires. By the time the men arrived on the scene, they were often too tired to put out the blaze.

Firefighting equipment from the late 1600s

By the 1850s, firemen started using steam-powered water pumps. The **steam engines** could weigh more than 8,000 pounds (3,629 kg). Some were too heavy for the men to pull, so strong horses were needed. By 1870, these four-footed firemen became important members of many fire departments.

Steam engines, such as this one, were too heavy for firefighters to pull themselves.

In 1832, a group of New York firemen bought the first horse to pull a ladder truck.

Choosing a Fire Horse

Getting firemen and equipment to a fire quickly took a special horse. A fire horse had to be strong enough to pull the heavy equipment. He had to have lots of energy to gallop long distances. The animal also needed to be able to run on rocky, muddy, or icy streets.

During the winter, a special sleigh was used to move easily over icy streets.

Even if a horse was powerful, he might not get the job. A fire horse needed to be brave when flames and ashes filled the air. The animal also needed to be calm since he worked near many loud noises. A horse that was easily scared might gallop away, hurting the firemen or damaging the equipment.

Three horses were often needed to pull the heavy steam engines and larger ladder trucks.

Both **stallions** and **mares** could be fire horses.

Training

Most fire horses learned to do their jobs by watching the trained horses work and then practicing. To practice getting hitched to the wagon, a fireman set off the alarm. Then two men led the horses from the stall to the front of the wagon. The horses stood under a **harness** that hung from the ceiling. It dropped onto their backs. Then a fireman closed the collars around their necks. If the horses stood still, they got treats. They did this again and again, until the horses knew where to stand.

The harness dropped from the ceiling to help the horses get quickly hitched to the wagon.

After the horses learned where to stand, the firemen tied a rope from the stall door to the front of the wagon. The horses learned to follow the rope to their place without the help of the firemen. With training, most horses were ready to work in less than two years.

Trained fire horses were often waiting at the wagon before the firemen even gathered.

Detroit, Michigan, was the only city to have a horse college to train fire horses. Horses received report cards to show their progress.

Daily Life

Fire horses began their day by 6:00 A.M. They got grain and hay for breakfast. If the horses had not responded to a fire within the past 24 hours, the **driver** hitched the team to a light wagon. He drove them a short distance to give them exercise. The animals did not work hard, though. They needed to save their energy in case there was a fire.

Horses love to eat hay. Some can eat 15 to 25 pounds (7 to 11 kg) a day.

When the horses finished their exercise, the driver **groomed** them. He brushed their coats and picked the stones out of their **hooves.** The animals stayed in their stalls for the rest of the day. At 6:00 P.M., the horses were given grain and hay for dinner.

Firehouses were home to both the horses and the men. There was a second floor where the men slept and relaxed.

At the Fire

Most firehouses had only one or two trucks or wagons. So several firehouses were built around towns to house the different kinds of equipment firefighters needed. When an alarm sounded, the firemen at each station harnessed their horses. The ladder trucks, hose wagons, and steam engines closest to the fire answered the call first. The equipment from other firehouses was used if the fire could not be put out quickly.

A ladder truck and a hose wagon leave a firehouse to tackle a fire in 1906.

Most fire stations were built less than two miles (3.2 km) apart. This short distance between stations allowed firemen to get to most fires in less than 6 minutes.

Once the firemen arrived, they unloaded the ladders and hoses. Then they moved the horses away from the flames. The horses that pulled the steam engines, however, walked as close to the fire as possible. Then the driver unhitched the team and led the horses away, leaving the steam engine. The horses stood still until the fire was put out.

During this fire in Baltimore, Maryland, the horses stood far away from the flames.

After the Fire

After helping put out a fire, the horses returned to the firehouse. The animals were usually hot and sweaty. To stay healthy, they needed to get their body temperatures back to normal. So the driver washed the horses with water and dried them. He then covered them with a blanket. The driver also cleaned out the horses' mouths to get rid of any dirt and ash. Then he removed stones and nails from their hooves.

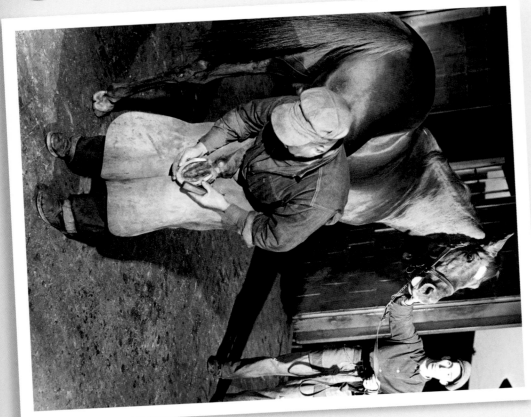

Horses' hooves grow like human fingernails. They need to be trimmed every six to eight weeks.

Drinking too much water can make a hot horse sick. So the fire horses were given only a few sips of water when they first returned to the firehouse.

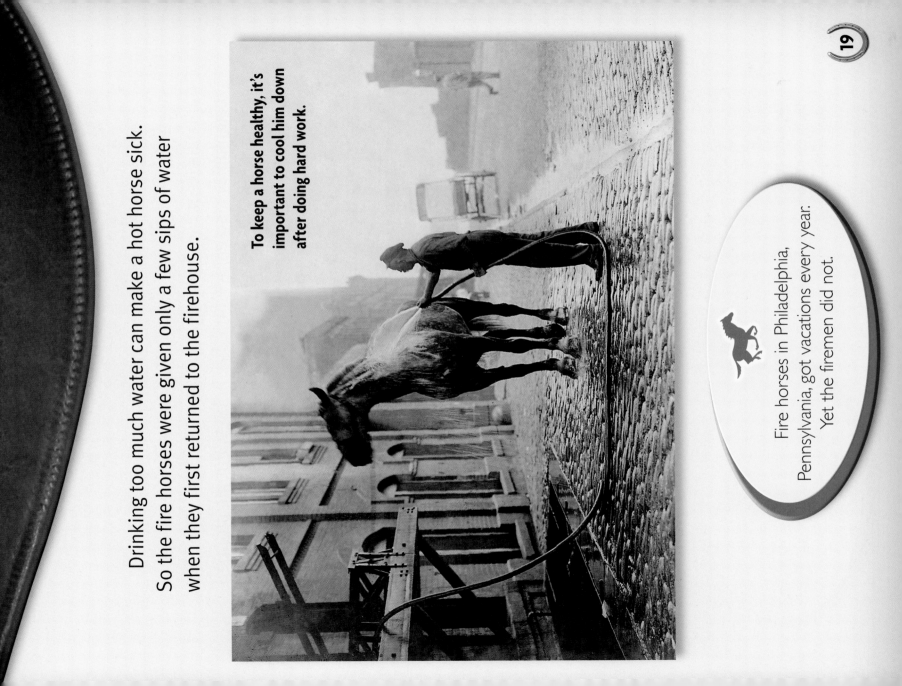

To keep a horse healthy, it's important to cool him down after doing hard work.

Fire horses in Philadelphia, Pennsylvania, got vacations every year. Yet the firemen did not.

Firehouse Pets

While the fire horses were working animals, they were also considered pets. The firemen often gave the animals treats such as sugar cubes and apples. The **community** also enjoyed the fire horses. People stopped by the firehouse to visit them. On the weekends, children got to ride in the wagons while the horses exercised.

Dogs, like this Dalmatian, ran near the horses to keep people and other animals away.

Many firehouses kept dogs as pets. They helped the horses stay calm.

Sometimes, fire horses, such as Bill and Doll, were allowed to roam around the firehouse. In the evenings, the two animals **trotted** to the front door of the firehouse. They watched the people in the city walk by. Bill and Doll stayed in the firehouse, though. They knew they had to be ready if the alarm sounded.

Some people in New York City visit with their neighborhood fire horses, Happy and Fairfax, in 1920.

Dangers on the Job

Since fire horses worked near flames, they often faced many dangers. Once, in 1905, a driver in the Los Angeles Fire Department took a steam engine too close to a burning store. Later, the driver saw that the horse closest to the flames had minor burns.

Sadly, this horse fell while racing to a fire.

In 1872, a disease caused many horses to become ill or die in the United States. So, the firemen and other people had to pull the fire equipment. During this time, a fire in Boston, Massachusetts, burned much of the city.

Leg injuries were common among fire horses. They often got hurt because they galloped too quickly while pulling heavy loads. In 1912, the Toledo Fire Department lost their most **dedicated** horse to a leg injury. Jim had answered eight calls in one day. When the ninth alarm sounded, Jim was standing on just three legs in front of the wagon. He had broken a leg and was unable to go to the fire.

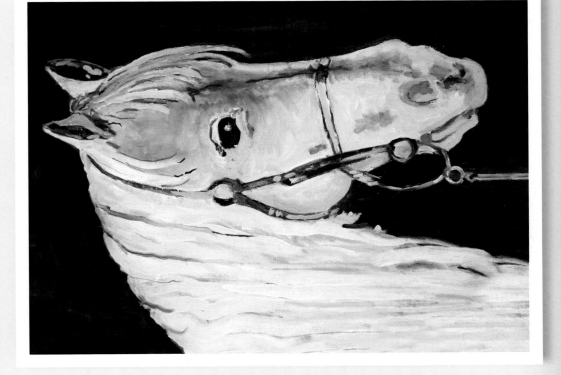

Jim was so well liked that the firemen had this portrait painted of him.

Retirement

Fire horses needed to be strong and quick. After four to ten years of work, most horses were not as powerful as they once were. At this time, fire departments sometimes **retired** them. Many were **auctioned** off. Some people bought the horses to pull delivery wagons.

People gather around two fire horses that are being auctioned off.

The fire horses never forgot their old jobs, though. Frank and Fox were fire horses in Missouri. After they retired in 1914, each began delivering milk for different companies. One day a fire alarm sounded. Both horses heard it and galloped toward the firehouse. They had forgotten that they were no longer fire horses.

Many retired fire horses pulled milk wagons such as this one in Madison, Wisconsin.

Jerry, a horse in Portland, Oregon, helped fight fires for 21 years, from 1890 to 1911.

Just a Memory

By 1906, **motorized** engines were commonly used in fire trucks. These engines could go faster and were cheaper to use than horses. They did not need hay and grain, which cost more than gas. By the mid-1920s, most firehouses had replaced horses with motorized equipment.

In 1922, these fire horses went out for one last gallop before being replaced with motorized vehicles.

As a result, horses like Bill and Doll were no longer needed. They were retired. In 1938, Doll was sold to a farmer. Bill, however, continued to live at the firehouse as its **mascot**. After more than 60 years of service, fire horses had at last become just a memory.

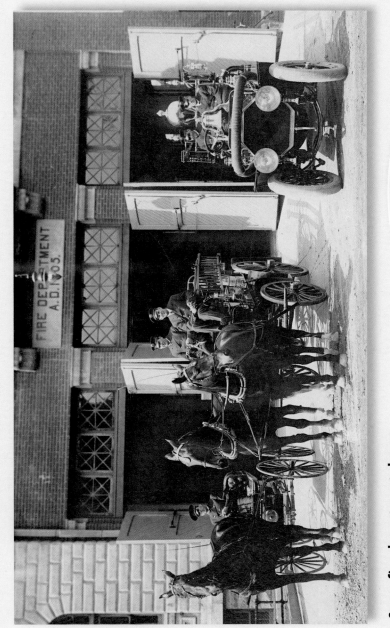

Some fire departments began to use motorized engines as early as 1899.

Bill served the Fredericton Fire Department for nine years. Even in retirement, when Bill heard the alarm, he raced to the new ladder truck and stood beside it.

FIRE DEPARTMENT
A.D. 1905.

Just the Facts

- Some horses got so excited at the sound of the fire alarm that they left without their driver. At a firehouse in Portland, Oregon, a horse-pulled steam engine left before the driver was in his seat. The horse raced to the fire. He waited by the **hydrant** until his driver arrived.

- Bill and Doll both liked to eat treats, such as sugar and apples. However, Bill liked to eat buttons best!

- Bill had a very good memory. One time a fireman gave him a lemon. Bill did not like the sour taste. From then on, he would not take another treat from the man, even if it was a candy bar.

- In 1902, a fire alarm sounded at the Toledo Fire Department. Fire horses Min and Mag took their places at the front of the steam engine. The harness dropped from the ceiling, and the collars closed around their necks. A fireman sat in his seat, forgetting to snap on the reins. As the horses galloped out the door, the driver realized he had no control of them. However, at top speed, Min and Mag drove through traffic and got the steam engine to the fire without the driver's help.

Common Breeds

Fire Horses

Suffolk Draft Horse

Percheron

Quarter Horse

Glossary

auctioned (AWK-shuhnd) sold to the person who offers the most money

community (kuh-MYOO-nuh-tee) a group of people who live together in the same place

dedicated (DED-uh-kayt-id) worked hard and faithfully

driver (DRYE-vur) the person who controls a wagon or truck

galloped (GAL-uhpt) ran at a very fast speed

groomed (GROOMD) washed, combed, and cared for

harness (HAR-niss) the straps that connect horses to the things they pull, such as wagons

hitched (HITCHT) attached to a wagon by a harness or ropes

hooves (HUVZ) the hard coverings over the feet of horses

hydrant (HYE-druhnt) a large outdoor pipe that is connected to a water supply

ladder truck (LAD-ur TRUHK) the truck that carried the ladders to the fires

mares (MAIRZ) female horses

mascot (MASS-kot) an animal, person, or thing that is used as a symbol for something else

motorized (MOH-tuh-rized) built with a motor that makes it run

patiently (PAY-shuhnt-lee) waiting calmly without getting upset

reins (RAYNZ) thin straps attached to the bridle that a driver holds to guide an animal

retired (ri-TYE-urd) stopped working, usually because of age

stall (STAWL) the area in a building where a horse is kept

stallions (STAL-yunz) male horses that can breed

steam engines (STEEM EN-juhnz) engines that used pressure from trapped steam to help shoot water at buildings

trotted (TROT-id) moved faster than a walk, but slower than a gallop

Bibliography

Ditzel, Paul C. *Fire Engines, Firefighters.* New York: Crown Publishers (1976).

Smith, Dennis. *Dennis Smith's History of Firefighting in America: 300 Years of Courage.* New York: Dial (1978).

www.frederictonfirefighters.ca/museum

www.lafire.com

www.toledofiremuseum.com/jimhorse/jimhorse.htm

Read More

Hatmon, Paul W. *Yesterday's Fire Engines.* Minneapolis, MN: Lerner Publications (1980).

Packard, Mary. *Working Horses.* New York: Bearport Publishing (2007).

Learn More Online

To learn more about fire horses, visit **www.bearportpublishing.com/HorsePower**

Index

About the Author

Margaret Fetty has written numerous children's books. She lives in Austin, Texas, where she enjoys running and biking.